EMERGENCY ROOM

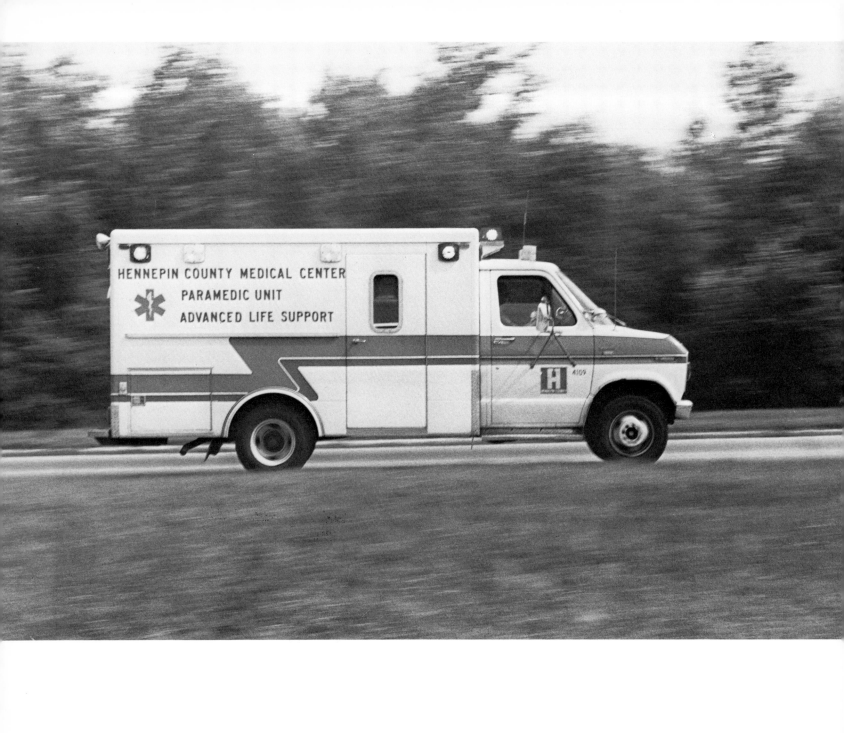

EMERGENCY ROOM

Bob and Diane Wolfe

Carolrhoda Books, Inc., Minneapolis

The authors would like to thank these special people who so generously shared their time and expertise to make this book possible: the St. Paul Ramsey Medical Center emergency room evening and night shift staffs and public relations staff, especially Robin Rainford and Becky Haus; the St. Paul fire department paramedics; and the Methodist Hospital (St. Louis Park, Minnesota) emergency room and public relations staffs, especially Karen Robideau and Betsy Becker.

A special thanks to paramedics Roger Sorenson and Al Mantie from Hennepin County Medical Center, Minneapolis, and to the people who shared their experiences with us: Jason Anderson, Scott Cohen, Neena Cohen, Denise Kennibrew, Andrew Lightowler, Gretchen Robideau, Mikey Roggenbuck, Rolf Stoylen, and Tom Wolfe.

LIBRARY OF CONGRESS CATALOGING IN PUBLICATION DATA

Wolfe, Robert L.
 Emergency room.

 Summary: Text and photographs describe activities occurring in a hospital emergency room as they follow a number of both seriously ill patients and patients with minor complaints through their treatment.
  1. Hospitals–Emergency service–Juvenile literature.
 [1. Hospitals–Emergency service] I. Wolfe, Diane.
 II. Title.
 RA975.5.E5W64 1983   616'.025   82-19878
 ISBN 0-87614-206-4 (lib. bdg.)

 2 3 4 5 6 7 8 9 10 92 91 90 89 88 87 86 85 84

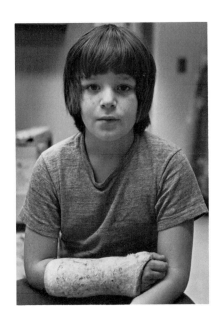

to our children, Joel and Joanne, and to Grandma Jayne, who over the years have provided us with several unforgettable trips to the emergency room

The emergency room, often called the E.R. for short, is a special place in a hospital where people can get medical help at any time of the day or night. Someone who has been hurt in a car accident may be rushed to the E.R. in an ambulance. Others may have been injured at home, at school, or on the job. They are often brought in by their families, friends, or police officers. Some people come to the emergency room because they are experiencing symptoms such as pain or fever. Even people with minor medical problems show up in the emergency room. Often their doctors are not in the office or it's late in the evening.

Of course, each hospital emergency room is a little different from any other, and, if you ever have to go to an emergency room, your experiences may not be exactly the same as those you read about here. But most emergency rooms are quite similar, and all of them are open twenty-four hours a day, seven days a week, to help you.

If you have to go to the emergency room, there are several different people who will take care of you. The E.R. doctor heads the team. Working with the doctor are experienced nurses, orderlies, and technicians. Interns (students who have just finished medical school) and residents (doctors who are continuing their medical education in a specialized area) work in the emergency room to continue their training and education. Everyone works under the supervision of an experienced doctor.

A full-time staff of ten doctors works in this emergency room, with residents filling in on weekends.

When you arrive at the E.R., you, your parent, or the person who brought you in will register you at the admitting desk. The admitting secretary will ask about your general health and medical background. He or she will also want to find out the details of your injury, such as how you were injured, where, and what time it happened. Your parents will be asked to fill out insurance forms and arrange to pay for your treatment in the emergency room.

Of course, a person with a life-threatening injury would be rushed to the emergency room and treatment would be started immediately. A family member or friend would have to take care of the admitting information.

Once you are registered, a plastic band with your name on it might be fastened around your wrist. This will identify you to all of the hospital staff.

It is possible that you will be treated immediately, but if your medical problem is minor, you may be asked to wait in the E.R. waiting room. Long waits are common here since more serious cases are taken care of first and may require a lot of time, so don't think that you have been forgotten.

Scott registers at the admitting desk.

It was early evening when Scott's mom brought him to the E.R. after he fell from a tree and injured his wrist. The pain and swelling indicated that it could be broken.

After he was admitted, a nurse took him to an examining room, helped him up on the examining table, then applied an ice pack to his swollen wrist. The cold ice keeps the injury from swelling more.

Next the nurse performed some routine tests that are given to all E.R. patients regardless of what is wrong with them. First she checked Scott's blood pressure. She wrapped a cuff around his upper arm, pumped it up with air until it felt tight, then slowly let the air out. As the pressure on Scott's arm decreases, the nurse is able to read his blood pressure by watching the pressure gauge attached to the cuff and listening to his pulse through a stethoscope. This test tells her how well Scott's heart is sending blood through his body.

Then the nurse took Scott's temperature. A high fever would be a sign of illness. A normal temperature is 98.6° F or 37° C. She also felt Scott's pulse to check the rate of his heartbeat.

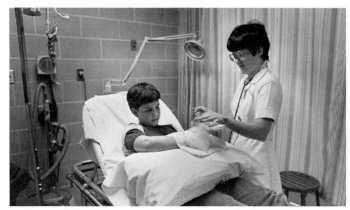

The nurse applies an ice pack to Scott's wrist.

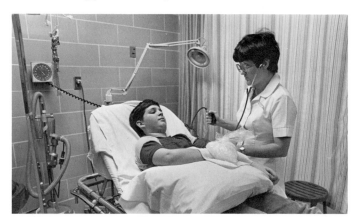

She checks Scott's blood pressure.

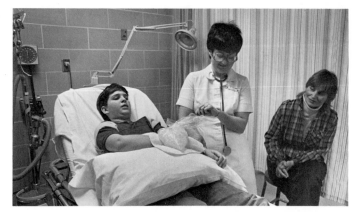

She feels Scott's pulse.

Next the nurse took Scott to the X-ray room where he was met by an X-ray technician, a specially trained person who positions the patient, operates the X-ray machine, and develops the X-ray film. The X-ray machine uses an electromagnetic ray which passes painlessly through the skin and records a picture of the bones on special X-ray film.

Once the X rays were taken, Scott had a short wait while the film was being developed. The technician wanted to make sure that she had gotten a good picture. If Scott hadn't been perfectly still when the X rays were being taken, the picture would be blurry and have to be reshot.

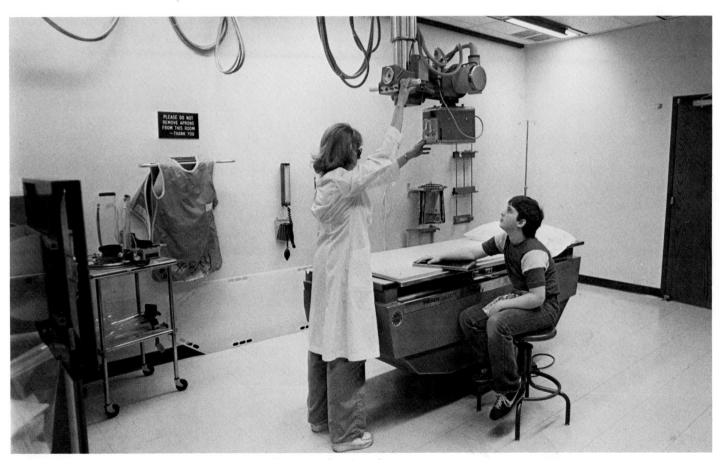

The X-ray technician positions the X-ray machine over Scott's wrist.

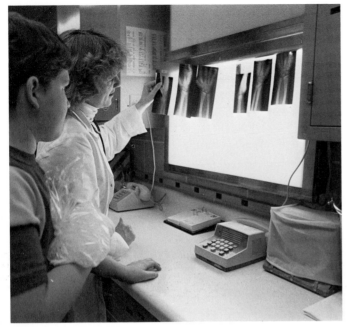
The doctor shows Scott his X rays.

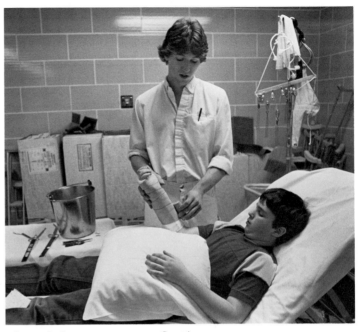
An orderly puts a cast on Scott's arm.

Scott's X rays came out fine, so the nurse took him back to the examining room where he and his mom met the doctor. The doctor asked about Scott's medical history, checked his injured arm, and looked at the X rays. The X rays told her exactly where and how badly Scott's bone was broken.

Scott's injury wasn't serious enough to require an operation (called surgery) to set his bone, but he would have to wear a cast to keep the bone in the correct position so that it could heal properly.

A trained nursing assistant, sometimes called an orderly, slipped a stocking-like material over Scott's arm. Then he dipped a plaster-coated bandage in water and wrapped it around the arm. As the bandage dried, it hardened and formed a cast.

The doctor advised Scott and his mother to see their family doctor in five days. The family doctor will take another X ray to see how well Scott's bone is healing. Scott's arm will have to remain in the cast until the bone is completely healed. This will take about five weeks.

A lot of cases that appear in the emergency room are due to sports accidents. Joel broke his finger while sparring in karate class. After he was admitted, the nurse took him to have it X rayed. You can see the crack in Joel's bone in the photograph of the X ray below.

The doctor used a splint to keep Joel's bone in place, then taped his fingers together to keep them from moving. Joel will have to visit an orthopedic surgeon (bone doctor) next week and have another X ray taken to make sure his finger is healing properly.

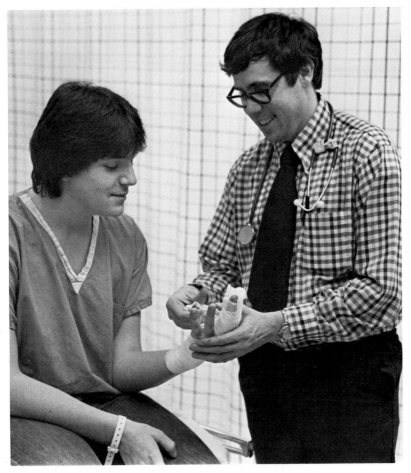

The doctor tapes Joel's fingers.

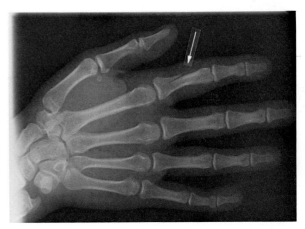

Joel's X ray

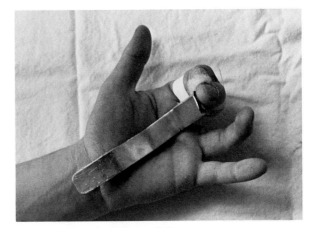

Joel's splinted and taped fingers

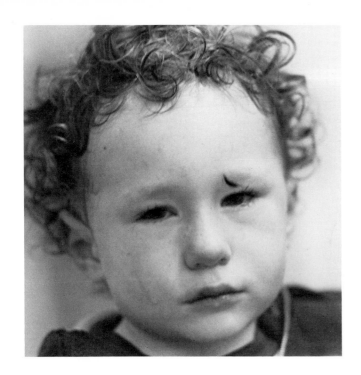

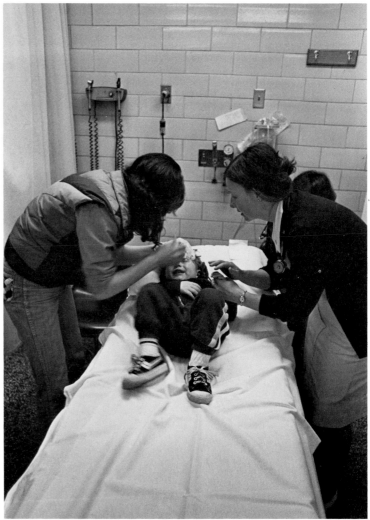

The nurse and Mikey's mother apply pressure
to stop the bleeding.

Mikey was brought to the emergency room after he fell and cut himself just above his eye. The nurse and his mother were able to stop the bleeding by applying direct pressure to the wound, but it was still necessary to close the cut with stitches. Stitches aid in the healing process and prevent a large scar from forming.

Because little Mikey's cut was so close to his eye and he was screaming and kicking, a special board was used to keep him still while the doctor sewed up his cut. He wasn't too happy about this, but it was necessary in order to avoid possible injury to his eye. Older children are more cooperative and usually don't need this restraint.

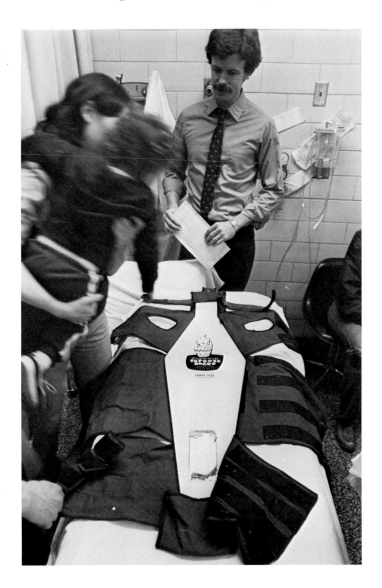
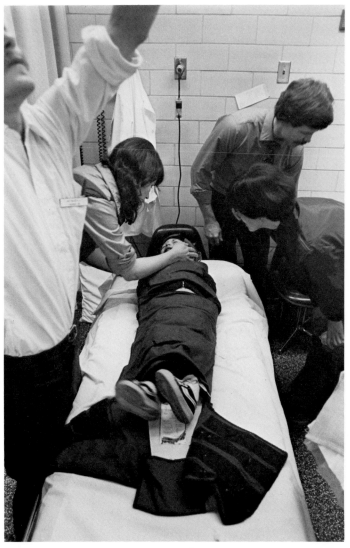

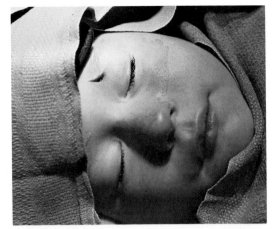

Mikey's wound is cleaned and draped.

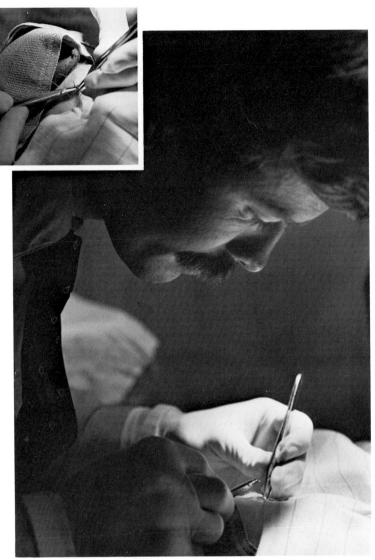

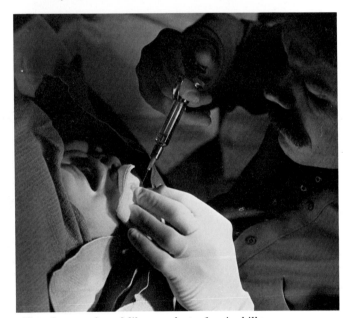

The doctor gives Mikey a shot of pain killer.

The doctor sutures Mikey's wound.

Mikey's wound was cleaned and the area was draped with sterile (germ-free) towels to prevent infection. Then the doctor gave Mikey a shot of pain killer so that it wouldn't hurt when the doctor sutured (stitched) the wound. Getting the shot hurt, but not for very long.

When the doctor had finished, the wound was cleaned again, and medicine was applied to prevent infection. Mikey was awake the whole time, but he kept his eyes closed because of the bright light.

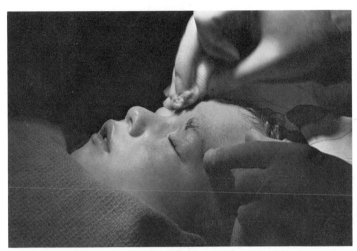
Mikey's wound is cleaned again.

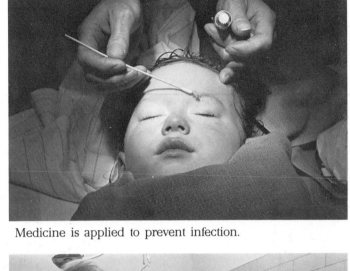
Medicine is applied to prevent infection.

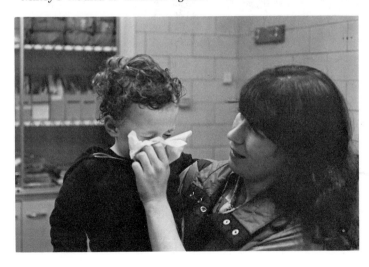

The nurse told Mikey's mother how to care for the wound until he could visit his family doctor to have the stitches removed.

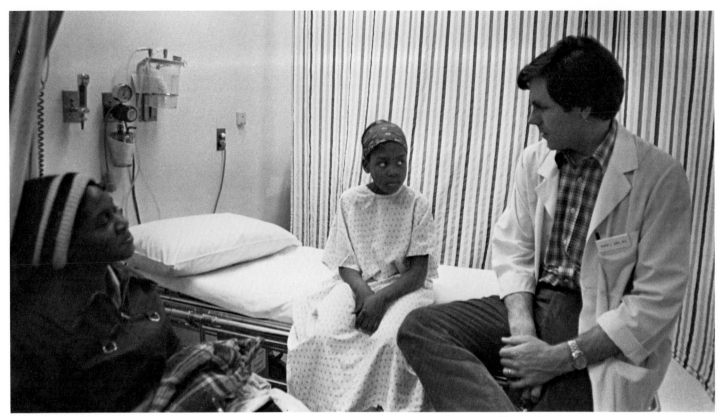

Dr. Jandal talks with Denise and her mother.

Late Friday night Denise's mother brought her to the emergency room. She was complaining of a sore throat, had a high fever, and was feeling miserable.

After they had registered with the admitting secretary, a nurse took Denise and her mother to a small examining room. She gave Denise an examining gown and told her to take off everything except her underwear. Once Denise had the gown on, the nurse returned to take her temperature, blood pressure, and pulse.

There was a knock on the door. It was Dr. Jandal. He came in to discuss Denise's symptoms with her mother. Then he told Denise that he would examine her and explained just what he would do.

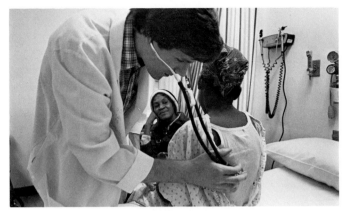

Dr. Jandal listens to Denise's heart and lungs.

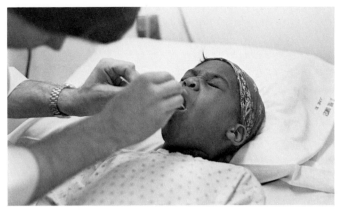

He takes a throat culture.

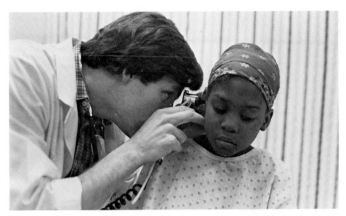

He examines her ears.

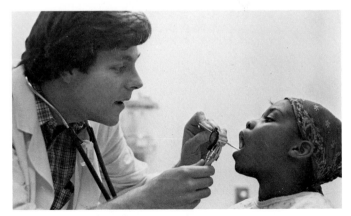

He examines her throat.

Using a stethoscope, Dr. Jandal listened to Denise's heart and lungs. They sounded fine. He examined her ears with an otoscope which lights and magnifies the inside of the ear. It tickled Denise a little bit, but it didn't hurt. Then Dr. Jandal lit up the back of Denise's throat with a small flashlight. He held her tongue down with a flat disposable stick, called a tongue depressor, so he could look at her throat.

Finally Dr. Jandal took a throat culture. This test may cause the patient to gag for a second, but it doesn't hurt. A cotton-tipped stick is rubbed around the back of the throat. It is then placed in a container and sent to the laboratory where it will be checked for bacterial growth to determine if an infection is present.

After finishing his examination, Dr. Jandal determined that Denise most likely had a virus. He prescribed medication and sent her home to bed.

Burns are a common sight in the emergency room. Some are more serious than others, but they are all painful. Burns can be caused by chemicals, electricity, powder (from guns, caps, or firecrackers), the sun, or, as in Gretchen's case, by touching something hot. Gretchen accidentally put her hand on a barbecue grill. Her mother immediately wrapped her hand in a clean towel packed with ice and brought her to the emergency room. The icepack helped to cool Gretchen's skin and prevent any further burning.

While Gretchen was soaking her hand in a pan of ice water, the nurse took her temperature, pulse, and blood pressure.

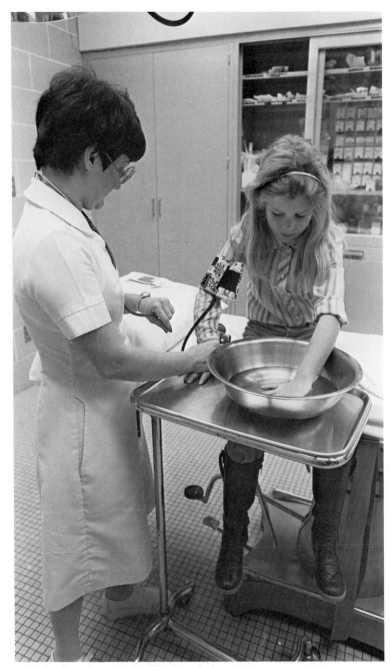

While Gretchen soaks her hand, the nurse takes her blood pressure.

Then she covered the burn with a special vaseline-coated bandage to protect it from infection. The nurse then wrapped Gretchen's hand with gauze to keep air away from the burn. Contact with the air would make the burn more painful.

Gretchen's hand will be sore for a few days, and she might have trouble moving it. She will also have to keep it dry.

Before Gretchen left the E.R. to go home, her mother was advised to see their family doctor in a few days. Their family doctor will check the burn for infection and decide if any further treatment is necessary.

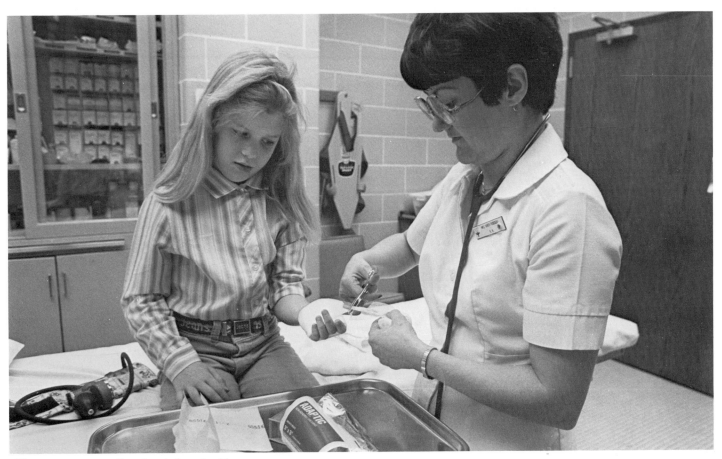

The nurse wraps Gretchen's hand with gauze.

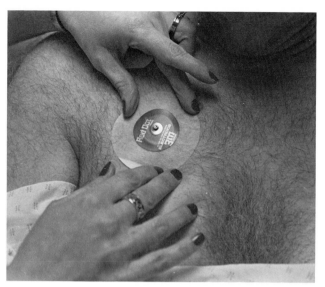

The nurse attaches an electrode ...

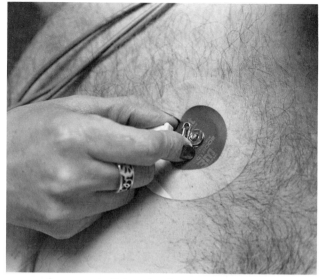

... and connects it to a lead.

Mr. Thomas came to the emergency room because he was suffering from chest pain, one of the warning signals of a heart attack. Immediately a nurse hooked him up to a cardiac (heart) monitor by attaching electrodes to his skin with an adhesive material. These electrodes pick up electrical impulses given off by the heart muscle. Each electrode is then connected by a lead (pronounced leed) to the cardiac monitor. The monitor then traces the rhythms of the heart on a screen much like a television screen.

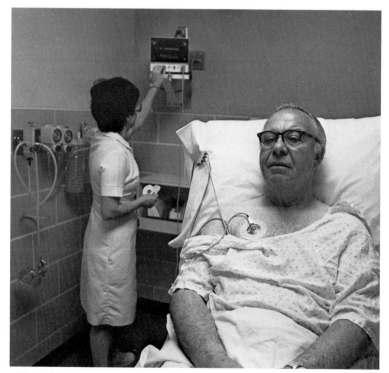

The nurse turns on the monitor.

Next an electrocardiogram (usually called an EKG) was taken by an EKG technician. Mr. Thomas was connected to a machine called an electrocardiograph in much the same way as he had been connected to the cardiac monitor. In this case the electrode and the lead are one unit. This unit is called a lead too. It is attached to the skin by a small rubber suction cup. The leads are then connected to a machine that electronically transmits the rhythm and force of each heartbeat. This information is recorded on graph paper and called an electrocardiogram. Both of these tests are painless.

After evaluating the tests and examining Mr. Thomas, the doctor determined that he was not having a heart attack but had torn a chest muscle while lifting a heavy box. He was sent home with orders to rest and to see his family doctor within the next few days.

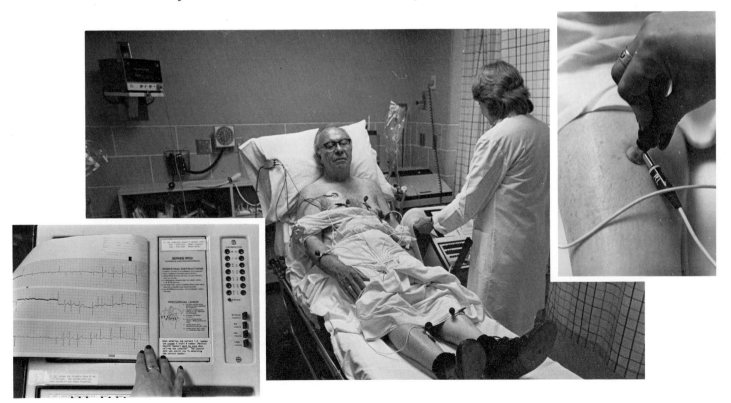

Hospital emergency rooms have a great deal of sophisticated equipment—they are ready for anything. This emergency room has a special area set aside for patients who are having difficulty breathing. It's called the Airway Board Room.

A person who has stopped breathing is in great danger. Unless oxygen is restored to his body within minutes, he can suffer brain damage or even die. Every effort must be made to restart his breathing. Extra oxygen can be given by placing an oxygen mask over the patient's face or inserting a tube just a little way into each nostril. These tubes are then connected to an oxygen tank which, when turned on, will force oxygen into the person's lungs.

Another instrument, called an airway, can be inserted into a patient's mouth and partway down his throat. This will keep his tongue from slipping back and blocking the air flow to his lungs.

If an object is caught in a person's throat, a tracheotomy will be performed. A small opening will be cut in the patient's windpipe and a tube, called a cannula, inserted. The cannula will bypass the object blocking the patient's throat and allow air into the windpipe so the patient can breathe.

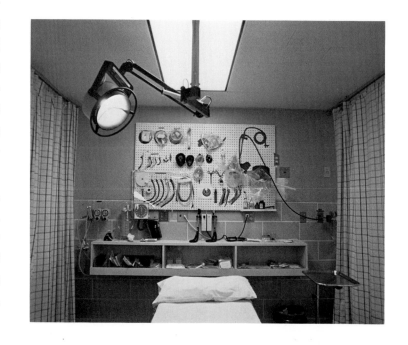

All of the instruments needed to perform these tasks are found hanging on the airway board located at the head of the patient's bed and within arm's reach of the doctor in the Airway Board Room.

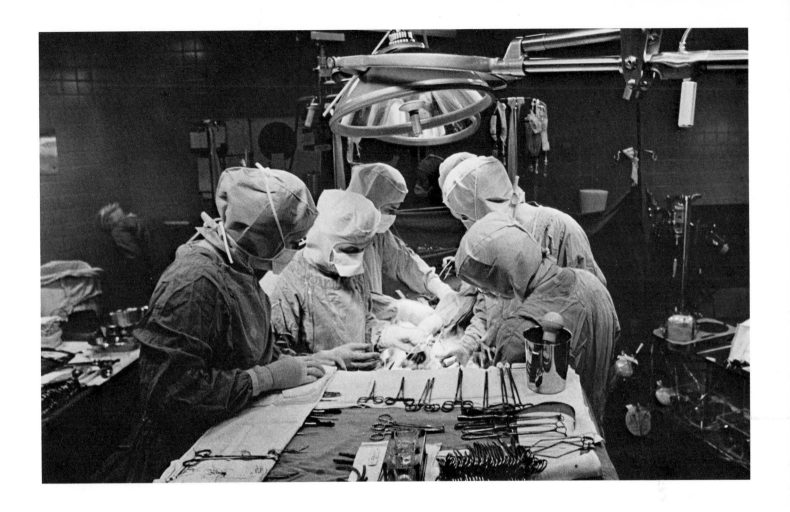

Many hospital emergency rooms also have a trauma team—a group of doctors, nurses, and technicians who are specially trained and equipped to deal with critical emergencies, such as gunshot wounds, where seconds count and immediate surgery is required. It was one such trauma team whose quick work and special training was a major factor in saving President Reagan's life.

Some hospitals also have special burn units. Severely burned patients can bypass the emergency room altogether and go directly to the burn unit for special treatment.

In extreme emergencies, when time could mean the difference between life and death, there is a team of highly trained professionals, called paramedics, who bring the emergency room to the patient.

These paramedics are treating a heart attack victim in his home. They immediately give him oxygen, take his blood pressure, and insert an IV needle into his vein. IV stands for intravenous, which means within (intra) the vein (venous). The IV is attached to a bag of liquid medication and allows the medication to go directly into the patient's bloodstream. An EKG is also taken.

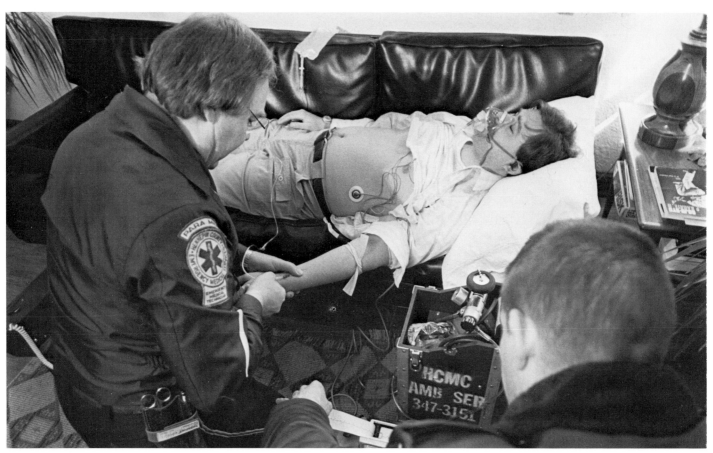

The paramedic inserts an IV needle into the patient's vein.

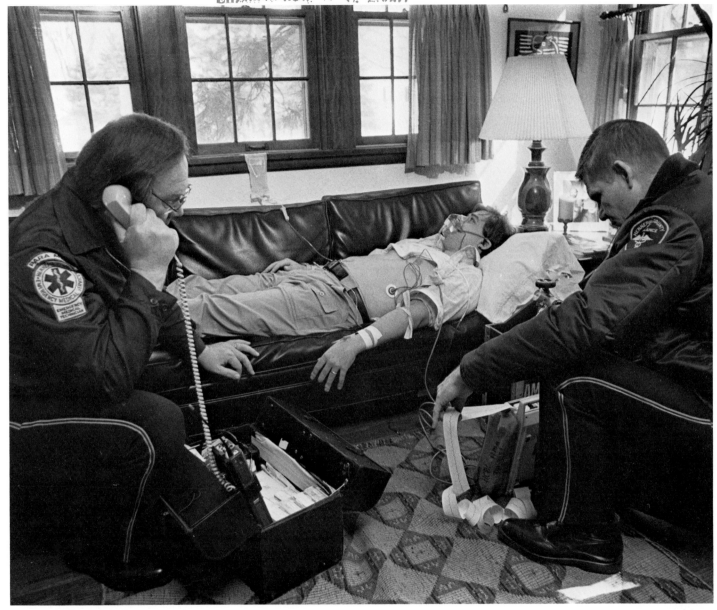

Then one of the paramedics contacts the emergency room doctor for instructions on further treatment.

The paramedics' EKG unit is connected to a similar unit in the emergency room so the doctor can read the patient's EKG immediately.

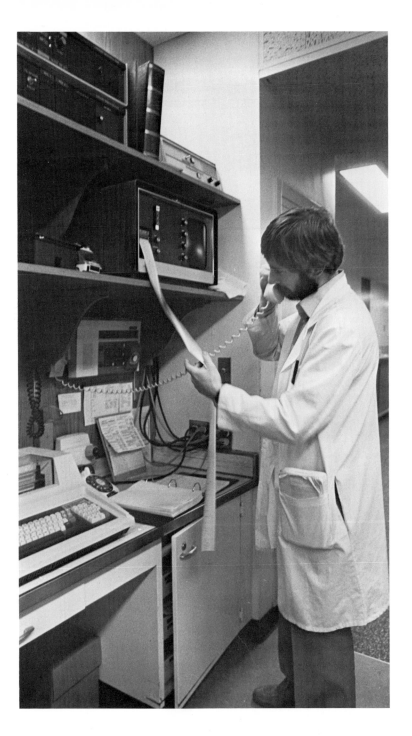

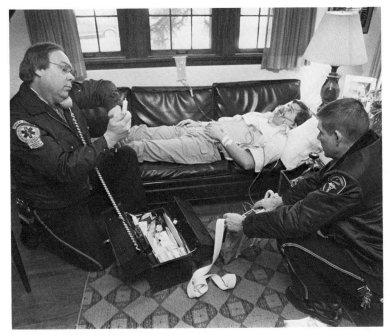

The paramedic gives further medication according to the doctor's instructions.

After receiving instructions from the doctor, the paramedics are able to administer appropriate further medication. Then they transport the patient by stretcher to the waiting ambulance. Within minutes he will be in the emergency room.

The paramedics transport the patient ...

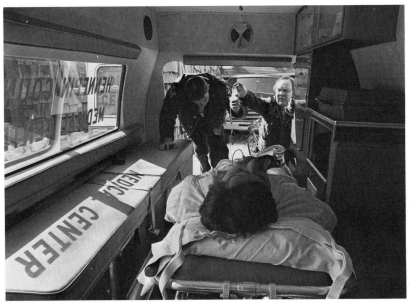

... to the waiting ambulance.

Jason was thrown from his bike when he was hit by a car. A neighbor notified the paramedics. When they arrived, they immediately checked Jason for life-threatening injuries. They made sure that he was breathing regularly, that his heartbeat was strong, and that he wasn't bleeding from the mouth or ears or suffering from other injuries. Jason didn't appear to have any broken bones, but the paramedics were concerned about the bump on his head.

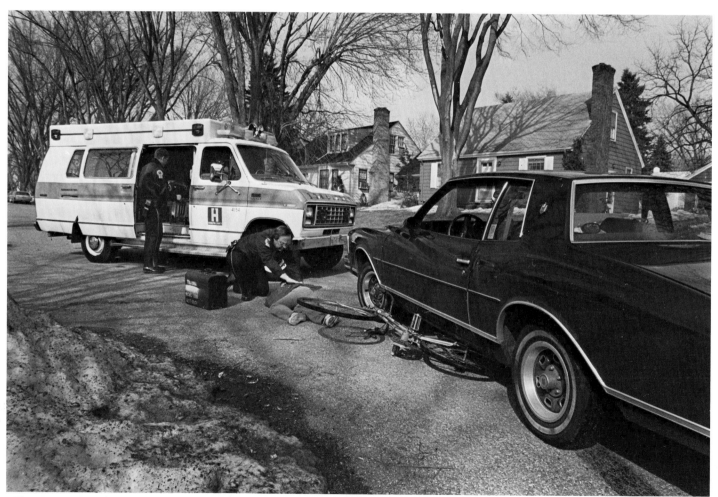

The paramedics immediately check Jason for any life-threatening injuries.

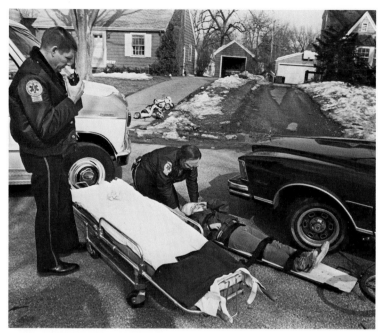

The paramedics notify the emergency room.

The emergency room doctor gives instructions.

They are quickly on their way to the hospital.

The paramedics notified the emergency room about Jason and reported that he might be suffering from a possible concussion. A concussion is a violent shock to or jarring of the brain and can be very dangerous. The doctor gave them instructions, and they were quickly on their way to the emergency room.

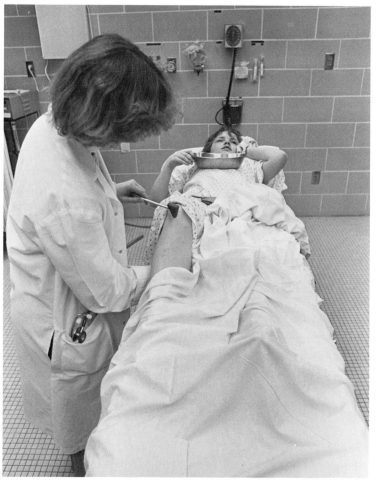

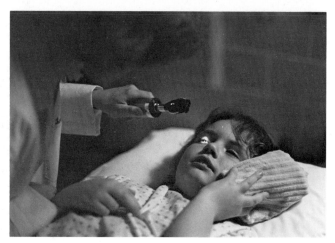

A few minutes later Jason arrived at the emergency room and was brought to an examining room. An ice pack was placed on his head injury to stop further swelling, and a doctor checked his reflexes for signs of a concussion. Reflexes, or responses, are checked to rule out damage to the brain. The eyes' reflex to light and the legs' reflex to stimulation are being checked in the photographs above.

Everything looked good for Jason, but he stayed in the hospital overnight for observation. He was able to go home the next day.

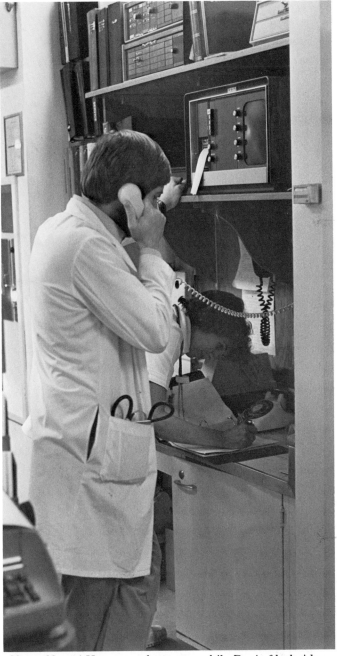
Nurse Naomi Hamann takes notes while Dr. Aufderheide receives the call.

It was 9:30 PM when Dr. Aufderheide received a call from the fire department rescue squad. They were on their way to the emergency room with a patient.

An elderly man had been eating dinner in a restaurant when he choked on a piece of meat. Several people came to his aid; one called the rescue squad. A bystander was able to dislodge the meat by using the Heimlich technique. This is done by wrapping your arms around the victim, slightly above the waist, and thrusting upward, but it can only be done by someone trained in the technique. The man lost consciousness and stopped breathing. That could have meant that he was having a stroke or a heart attack, or that insufficient oxygen was getting to his brain because of the piece of meat he had choked on. In any case, his breathing had to be restored quickly. A bystander started cardiopulmonary resuscitation, often called CPR for short. This is a combination of artificial respiration and artificial circulation. Like the Heimlich technique, it can only be done by a trained person. When the rescue squad paramedics arrived, they took over the CPR. The victim regained consciousness and started breathing on his own. An IV was started, a heart monitor connected, and oxygen was given to assist the patient in breathing. Once he was somewhat stabilized, he was loaded into the ambulance, and within minutes he arrived at the E.R.

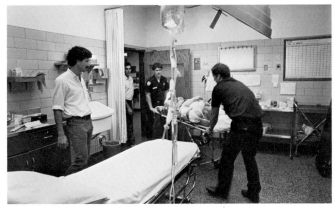

The patient is wheeled into Room 10.

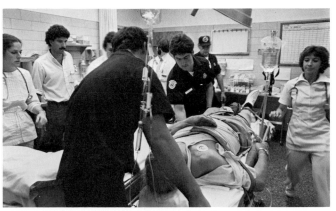

Immediately the room fills with medical staff.

Immediately the room filled with nurses, doctors, paramedics, and technicians. Dr. Aufderheide got as much information about the patient as he could from the paramedics, and everyone got busy checking the patient's vital signs and drawing blood samples to check things like his blood type and blood sugar level.

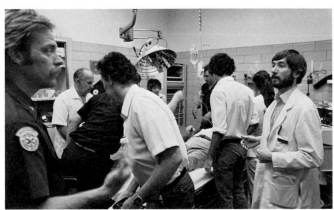

Dr. Aufderheide gets information from the paramedics.

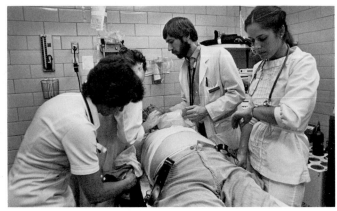

The patient's pulse and blood pressure are checked.

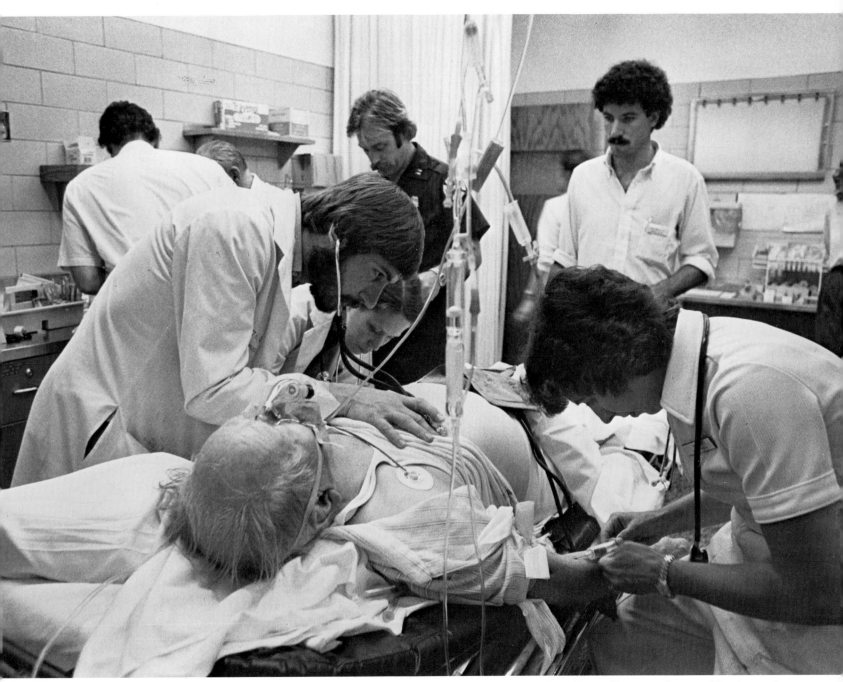

Dr. Aufderheide listens to the patient's heart and lungs while Nurse Hamann draws a blood sample.

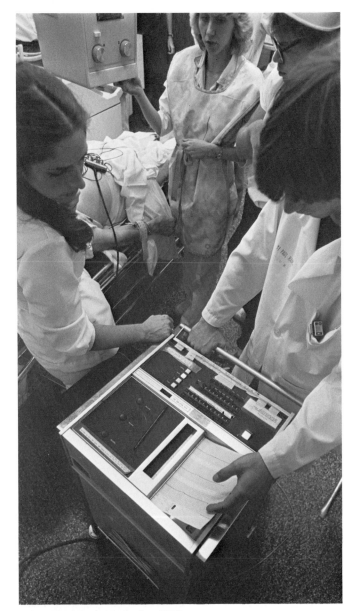

A technician reads the EKG.

A portable X-ray machine is wheeled into Room 10.

The patient was connected to an EKG machine to make sure he was not having a heart attack.

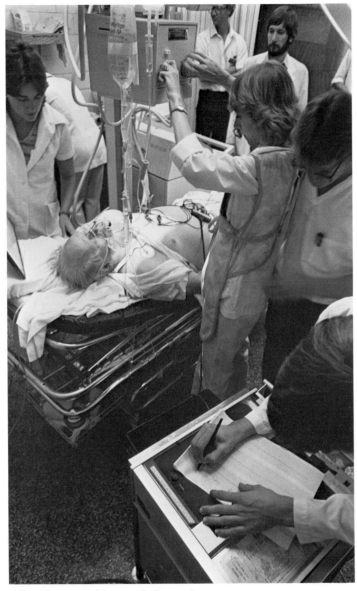

The X-ray machine and the patient
are positioned for the X ray.

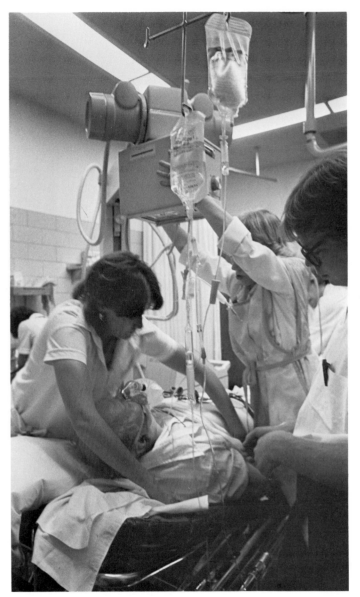

A technician prepares to slide the X-ray
film underneath the patient.

Then, using a portable X-ray machine, X rays were taken to make certain
one of the patient's lungs hadn't collapsed during CPR.

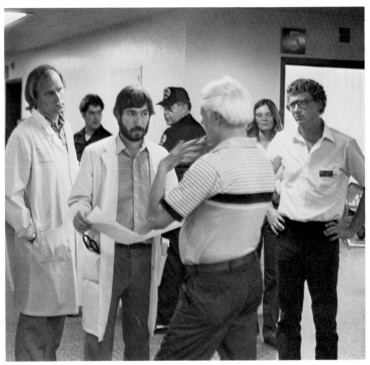

Dr. Aufderheide talks with the patient's friend.

Dr. Aufderheide stepped into the hallway to speak to the patient's friend who had been eating dinner with him at the restaurant and accompanied him to the hospital. He asked the friend to describe exactly what had happened.

By the time they had finished talking, the X rays had been developed, and Dr. Aufderheide went to look at them. The patient's lungs looked fine.

Dr. Aufderheide looks at the X rays.

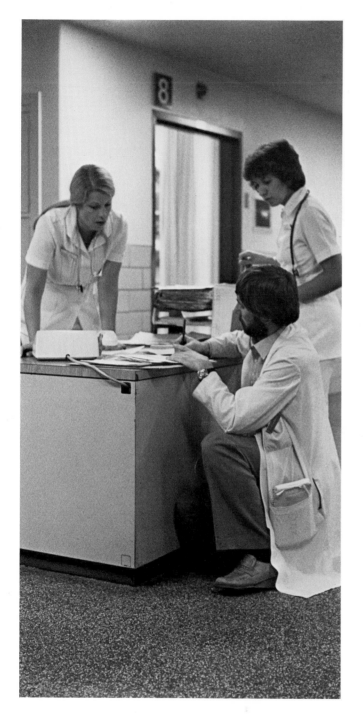

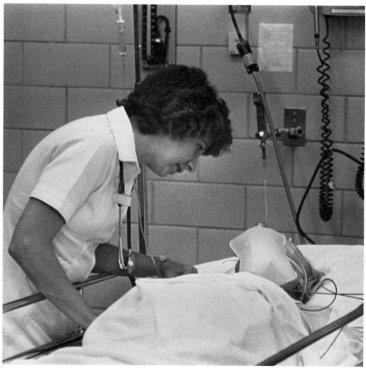

While Dr. Aufderheide wrote information and instructions on the patient's chart, nurse Naomi Hamann was reassuring the patient that he was doing well, that his family had been notified, and that he would be admitted to the hospital's critical care unit (C.C.U.) for observation.

Although most of us will never have to go to the emergency room for a critical problem like the last patient's, many of us have been or will go to the emergency room with less serious problems. But no matter what our problems are, it is comforting to know that there is a place open day and night where we can find help in a medical emergency.

C. 2

J
616
W

Wolfe, Robert L.

Emergency room